JR. GRAPHIC MONSTER STORIES

VAMPIRES!

STEVEN ROBERTS

PowerKiDS
press
New York

Published in 2013 by The Rosen Publishing Group, Inc.
29 East 21st Street, New York, NY 10010

First Edition

Editor: Joanne Randolph
Book Design: Planman Technologies
Illustrations: Planman Technologies

Library of Congress Cataloging-in-Publication Data

Roberts, Steven.
Vampires! / by Steven Roberts. — 1st ed.
    p. cm. — (Jr. graphic monster stories)
Includes index.
ISBN 978-1-4488-7906-9 (library binding) — ISBN 978-1-4488-8006-5 (pbk.) — ISBN 978-1-4488-8012-6 (6-pack)
1. Vampires—Juvenile literature. I. Title.
BF1556.R59 2013
398'.45—dc23

                        2011047508

Manufactured in the United States of America
CPSIA Compliance Information: Batch # SW12PK: For Further Information contact Rosen Publishing, New York, New York at 1-800-237-9932

Contents

Main Characters

Johannes Fluckinger (c. 1730s) Austrian surgeon who wrote a famous report to the Austrian emperor about the vampire plague in Medvegia, Serbia.

Emperor Francis I (1708–1765) Ordered the surgeon Johannes Fluckinger to investigate the mysterious vampire plague in Medvegia, Serbia. Francis I received the written report from Fluckinger on vampirism that became well-known throughout Europe.

Arnold Paole (c. 1710–1727) A soldier who became a vampire while serving in the Austrian army. It was thought that Arnold started a vampire plague in his hometown of Medvegia, Serbia.

Vampires!

JANE, EMILY, AND CHARLOTTE GOT TOGETHER FOR JANE'S BIRTHDAY. THEY MET AT CHARLOTTE'S HOUSE.

HAPPY BIRTHDAY, JANE!

THANKS FOR THE VAMPIRE BOOK . . . LOOKS INTERESTING. DO YOU USUALLY READ THIS STUFF, CHARLOTTE?

OH, YES! I LOVE **VAMPIRE** BOOKS. I WISH I COULD MEET A *REAL* VAMPIRE!

THERE'S NO SUCH THING AS A REAL VAMPIRE, SILLY.

ACTUALLY . . . I READ A BOOK ABOUT A REAL VAMPIRE. HAVE YOU EVER HEARD OF ARNOLD PAOLE?

"ARNOLD PAOLE WAS A SOLDIER IN THE AUSTRIAN ARMY IN THE 1700S."

FIRE!

"AFTER FIGHTING IN THE ARMY, PAOLE RETURNED TO HIS HOMETOWN OF MEDVEGIA, SERBIA.

"PAOLE BOUGHT SOME LAND AND SETTLED DOWN TO FARM.

"PAOLE'S NEIGHBORS NOTICED THERE WAS SOMETHING TROUBLING HIM. PAOLE TOLD THEM ABOUT A TERRIBLE THING THAT HAD HAPPENED TO HIM IN THE ARMY."

WHAT IS THE MATTER, ARNOLD?

I AM CURSED!

"PAOLE DESCRIBED AN EXPERIENCE HE HAD WHEN HE WAS A SOLDIER. ONE NIGHT WHILE ON GUARD DUTY, PAOLE SAW A FIGURE IN THE WOODS."

WHO GOES THERE?

"AS HE APPROACHED THE FIGURE, IT SUDDENLY **ATTACKED** HIM!"

SCREEEEECH!

"PAOLE FOUGHT OFF THE **CREATURE**."

EEEEEK!

"WHEN PAOLE RECOVERED, HE CHASED IT THROUGH THE WOODS."

CREATURE, WHAT ARE YOU?

"HE CAUGHT UP TO THE CREATURE."

HISSSSSS!

"PAOLE MANAGED TO KILL THE CREATURE . . . BUT NOT BEFORE IT BIT HIM ON THE NECK."

ARGHHHH!

"PAOLE AND THE FARMERS KNEW WHAT HAD ATTACKED HIM."

IT WAS A *VAMPIRE!*

"A FEW WEEKS LATER, PAOLE DIED AFTER HE FELL WHILE WORKING ON HIS FARM."

"PAOLE WAS BURIED THE NEXT DAY. HIS NEIGHBORS FORGOT HIS UNBELIEVABLE STORY."

MAY ARNOLD PAOLE REST IN PEACE.

"A **PANIC** SPREAD THROUGHOUT THE TOWN. THE TOWNSPEOPLE TOOK PAOLE'S **CASKET** FROM ITS TOMB TO **EXAMINE** THE BODY.

PAOLE'S BODY WAS PERFECTLY **PRESERVED**. HE LOOKED AS IF HE WERE ASLEEP. HOWEVER, HIS HAIR AND FINGERNAILS HAD GROWN.

"WHEN THEY PRICKED HIS SKIN WITH A NEEDLE, BLOOD CAME OUT."

HE BLEEDS! THIS PROVES THAT ARNOLD IS A VAMPIRE!

"CONVINCED THAT PAOLE WAS A VAMPIRE, THE TOWNSPEOPLE DROVE A STAKE THROUGH HIS HEART AND BURNED HIS BODY TO MAKE SURE HE WAS DEAD.

"THEY STAKED AND BURNED THE BODIES OF THE FOUR PEOPLE WHO DIED AFTER SEEING PAOLE. THEY THOUGHT THEY, TOO, HAD BECOME VAMPIRES.

"FOR A WHILE, LIFE RETURNED TO NORMAL IN THE VILLAGE.

BEEF FOR SALE

"FIVE YEARS LATER, SOME PEOPLE IN THE TOWN CAME DOWN WITH A MYSTERIOUS ILLNESS."

BEEF FOR SALE

I FEEL ILL.

"WITHIN A THREE-MONTH PERIOD, 17 PEOPLE SUDDENLY BECAME SICK AND DIED.

"NEWS OF THE OUTBREAK REACHED THE EMPEROR IN AUSTRIA. FEARING THE **PLAGUE**, HE SENT ARMY SURGEON JOHANNES FLUCKINGER TO **INVESTIGATE**."

YOU MUST STOP THIS PLAGUE BEFORE IT SPREADS!

YES, YOUR MAJESTY!

"DR. FLUCKINGER WENT IMMEDIATELY TO MEDVEGIA.

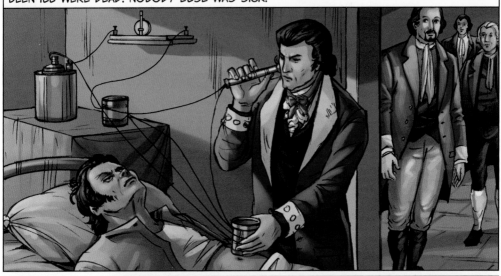

"DR. FLUCKINGER EXAMINED MANY OF THE TOWNSPEOPLE, BUT THE PEOPLE WHO HAD BEEN ILL WERE DEAD. NOBODY ELSE WAS SICK."

"NOBODY KNEW WHAT TO MAKE OF THE OUTBREAK. THEN A YOUNG WOMAN CAME FORWARD."

A MAN ATTACKED ME LAST NIGHT NEAR MY HOME. IT WAS MILO, MY OLD FRIEND FROM THE VILLAGE.

"THE MEN WERE TERRIFIED."

MILO HAS BEEN *DEAD* FOR THREE WEEKS!

THEN MILO IS A VAMPIRE!

"DR. FLUCKINGER ORDERED MILO'S GRAVE OPENED SO HE COULD EXAMINE THE BODY. HE FOUND IT IN THE SAME STATE THAT ARNOLD PAOLE'S BODY HAD BEEN IN FIVE YEARS EARLIER."

"THE DOCTOR IMMEDIATELY ORDERED THE BODY STAKED AND BURNED."

WE MUST DESTROY THESE EVIL CREATURES!

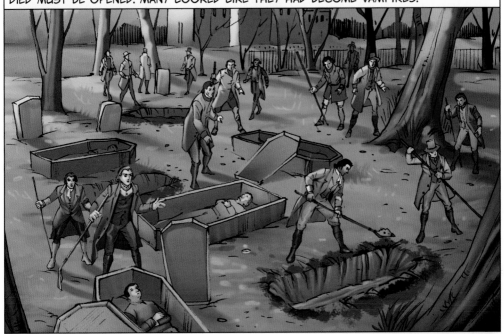

"THE DOCTOR THEN ORDERED THAT ALL THE GRAVES OF PEOPLE WHO HAD RECENTLY DIED MUST BE OPENED. MANY LOOKED LIKE THEY HAD BECOME VAMPIRES.

"ALL OF THE BODIES WERE STAKED AND BURNED.

"THE TOWNSPEOPLE WERE FRIGHTENED AND CONFUSED."

HOW COULD THIS HAVE HAPPENED?

IT HAS BEEN FIVE YEARS SINCE WE STAKED AND BURNED ARNOLD!

"DR. FLUCKINGER WANTED TO FIND THE CAUSE OF THE NEW OUTBREAK. HE SPOKE TO THE LOCAL **BUTCHER.**

"THE DOCTOR ALSO TALKED TO THE VILLAGE **TAVERN** KEEPER.

"DR. FLUCKINGER MADE A SURPRISING **DISCOVERY.** ALL OF THE PEOPLE WHO RECENTLY DIED HAD EATEN MEAT FROM CATTLE ONCE OWNED BY THE VAMPIRE ARNOLD PAOLE.

"THE DOCTOR CONCLUDED THAT PAOLE HAD BEEN FEEDING ON THE BLOOD OF HIS COWS.

"THE COWS THEN BECAME **INFECTED**. WHEN SOME OF THE TOWNSPEOPLE ATE MEAT FROM THE COWS, THEY BECAME INFECTED, TOO, AND TURNED INTO VAMPIRES."

OOOOH!

More Vampire Stories

- **Countess Elizabeth Bathory**
  Elizabeth Bathory lived in the late 1500s in Austria-Hungary. As a child, she behaved strangely. She could not control her temper and often flew into a rage over minor things. As an adult, she was extremely cruel to her servants. She would force them to go outside in the winter with little or no clothing. She stuck needles under their fingernails and tortured them in other ways. Eventually, Bathory made the mistake of killing a noblewoman. This got the attention of the authorities, and Bathory was arrested. She was tried for crimes involving more than 650 victims. She was accused of being a vampire. It was said that she drained the blood from the bodies of many of her victims and bathed in it. She claimed this was the secret of her beauty.

- **Peter Plogojowitz**
  Peter Plogojowitz lived in Serbia. He died in 1725. Within a few days of his death, nine people in his village claimed to have been attacked by him. Soon all nine of these people died of different causes. Peter's wife claimed that he came to her home and asked their son for food. When the son refused, Peter killed him. The villagers opened up Peter's casket to check the corpse, fearing that he was a vampire. The villagers staked Peter's body and burned it.

- **The Vampire of Berwick**
  The legend of the Berwick vampire comes from the 1100s in northern England. Residents became fearful when a man who had recently died was seen walking through town. His presence made the dogs in the town howl through the night. The hysterical townspeople removed the man's body from its grave, cut it in pieces, and burned it. Shortly thereafter, a disease swept through the town, killing many people. It was thought that this disease sprung from the recent presence of the vampire.

Glossary

attacked (uh-TAKD) Tried to hurt someone or something.

butcher (BU-cher) A person who prepares meat for people to buy and eat.

casket (KAS-ket) A long box that holds a dead person who is to be buried.

creature (KREE-chur) A person or animal.

discovery (dis-KUH-vuh-ree) Something that has been found for the first time.

disease (dih-ZEEZ) An illness or sickness.

examine (ig-ZA-mun) To look closely at something.

figure (FIH-gyur) The form or shape of a person.

infected (in-FEK-ted) Became sick from germs.

investigate (in-VES-tuh-gayt) To try to learn the facts about something.

panic (PA-nik) A sudden feeling of fear.

plague (PLAYG) A very bad illness.

preserved (prih-ZURVD) Kept from decaying, or going bad.

rabies (RAY-beez) A deadly illness that wild animals can carry.

tavern (TA-vurn) A place to spend the night and eat a meal.

tomb (TOOM) A grave.

vampire (VAM-py-er) A dead person from stories and folktales who sucks the blood of living people.

Index

Websites

Due to the changing nature of Internet links, PowerKids Press has developed an online list of websites related to the subject of this book. This site is updated regularly. Please use this link to access the list:

www.powerkidslinks.com/mons/vamp/